The Fugitive
Sunshine

The Fugitive Sunshine

Selected Poems

SYEDA AFSHANA

PARTRIDGE
A Penguin Company

Partridge books may be ordered through booksellers or by contacting:

Partridge India
Penguin Books India Pvt.Ltd
11, Community Centre, Panchsheel Park, New Delhi 110017
India
www.partridgepublishing.com
Phone: 000.800.10062.62

CONTENTS

Foreword   xiii
Terms   xvii

Time And Life   1
Me And I   4
A Companion   6
Oscillations   8
Dark Room   10
Lame Time   12
Realities   14
Thank You, God!   15
Trade of Relations   17
A Flight   19
Utopia   21
A Silver Lining   24
A Wanton Fury   26
Antidote   28
Bear   29
But Perhaps   30
Her Soul   32
A Far Cry   33
A Scream   35
Fidelity   37
Another Dark Night   39
Stormy Lethe   42
The Waterloo   44
Reminder   46

Unknown Voice	48
Return Of Phoenix	50
All Blood, No Snow	54
Seesaw	59
Future of The Past	60
Motherly Verse	63
A Murmur Within	66
Winters Voice	69
Keep Going	74
Do's and Don'ts	76
A Mirage	78
Broken Idols	80
Nonchalance	85
Dream Portrait	87
My Songs	91
A Fresh Verve	93
A Pyrrhic Victory	95
Silent Talk	97
Déjà Vu	99
Radio Kashmir	101
A Swan song	103
Anonymity	105
A Dilemma	107
Page of Blood	109
Coalesce	111
City of Death	113
Antithesis	116
Retreat	118
Sulaiman	120

I dedicate this book
to my dear parents

This is the song of the downing day
And the ending night. Listen to it.
And from the harsh suffering,
Let the confident voice emerge.
                              (Pablo Neruda)

A word

The lines jotted down in this book
are simply a gift of God to me,
nothing else.
I am not a poet yet,
simply a novice.

(Syeda Afshana)

FOREWORD

I have been admiring Afshana's poems since she made her first girlish attempts to run after the eerie words, jingling rhymes, and the moral lessons. Since then there has been a continuous growth in the making of the poetess in her. Now when in the poems included in *The Fugitive Sunshine* there is the burden of experience and protest that Afshana wants to give vent, I am tempted to sing a hymn of celebration to Afshana's very attempt to represent herself; she amply deserves it. Though it was a great woman saint-poet namely Lal Dyad of the fourteenth century who founded the tradition of poetry in Kashmir, Kashmiri woman, throughout the dark centuries of feudalism and foreign rule depended on men for their representation. And what the male poets represented of the woman was a grotesque combination of some descriptive shibboleths like *shahmar zulf* (serpentine curls), *anznyi gardan* (a swan's neck), *bumi kaman* (bow shaped eyebrows), and so on and so forth. This cap-a-pie description of the dehumanized female body always resulted in bathos and hackneyed porno. Now when some young women of Kashmir like Afshana bravely venture to represent themselves, man's concept of womanhood is bound to change and women, too, have to get rid of the fallacies that have been invented by men and accepted by women as the truth about them.

What does Afshana really represent of herself? In the given socio-political milieu, we cannot expect more than a feeble attempt situating her being in various actualities as a being that cannot be taken as for granted. Her very stance of resentment and dismay is her revolt against the ill-state of woman that over six thousand years' history has reduced her into. Nevertheless, in spite of her situating herself in the world of things, Afshana is content with stretching herself in all her poems as an immanent existence: mute, still and passive like mother earth . . .

> But I was what I am now,
> A blithe and blest earthling,
> Accepting whatever I am given,
> Returning whatever I receive. *(A Far Cry)*

Afshana generally uses rumination as the generative principle of imagination and as a linear narrative is not possible: sensations, feelings, and observations are mingled with dream images, statements, and allusions. Many a time, she deliberately punctuates the narrative by intermittent silence.

It is in silence that she tries to articulate her protest. In "Motherly Verse" she raises her voice against the cultural determination of womanhood and the time-honored notions of female virtue. Though she is acutely quizzical about the political agendas, manifestoes and slogans, the overtones of the present political predicament are everywhere in her poems: her poems, being inalienable from her times, are a silent, but an effective protest against the macabre conditions that have overwhelmed this small Himalayan state because of the machinations of the global power(s). She, however, having an ambivalent relation with politics, protests in the form of passionate woman's lament for the thousands of the best of our youth. Her poems like "Stormy Lethe", "Reminder", "Unknown Voice", "All Blood, No Snow", "Pyrrhic Victory" and "Winter's voice" depict the agony and the perdition of the Kashmiri people.

Despite her unequivocal stance, Afshana as an artist eschews details as details not only abnegate her ontological being, but also mar the intensity of the experience, which is essentially brief.

> I evanesce into
> mists of alphabets
> lost in the
> dissipated details. *(Coalesce)*

The poems presented here intimate Afshana's growing disillusionment of the traditional verbal medium.

Prof. Shafi Shauq
(University of Kashmir,
Srinagar)

TERMS

Afsoos duniya kahsina lug samsaar sethi	Alas! world is not everlasting for anyone
Char Chinari	Small square shaped island with four Chinar trees on its corners in Dal Lake
Hammam	Ablution and heating system in the mosque
Hari-Parbat	Name of hill overlooking Srinagar
Hello Farmayish	A popular phone-in music program from Radio Kashmir
Kuch Kuch Hota Hai	Title song of popular Bollywood movie made in 90s
Marvati car	One of the cars manufactured by Maruti Suzuki pronounced as 'Marvati' by layman in Kashmir

Power Ka Sawaal hai	Question of power
Rasm-e-Chahrum	Fourth day death ceremony
Sulaiman	The hill, known as *Takt-i-Sulaiman,* overlooks Srinagar, the summer capital of Kashmir; standing 1000 feet above the plain
'Wakht Aosus Wotmut'	His time was up
Walo ha baaghvaanoa naw baharuk nav paida ker	Come O gardener! create glory of a new spring
Yaar, yeh second-hand maal hai	Dear, this is a second-hand item
Zainakadal	Bridge in the downtown of Srinagar

Time And Life

Hush of silence enshrouding a modest room
With fair curtains drawn,
Simple lights switched on
Unwillingly illumine a clock
Hanging on a wall, Once badly broken
Nevertheless somehow working
To break the ice
By its faint ticking beats.

Straight beneath it someone bed-ridden
With closed eyes,
Agitating fingers and
Frequent deep breaths,
Meditating over the past
Cudgelling the brains.

Reopening many old sores
And a few palmy days
Of an onerous life
Torn up by rents of poverty
And
Stitched up by thread of survival
Which was be-all and end-all.

Childhood of scarcity
Youth of hardships
Oldness of insalubrity
With rare commas of joy
And ubiquitous full-stops of grief
Composed the chapter of life,
A moving laborious life
Which at present
Had taken a halt
And parked itself at a place
Where tears and smiles
Pain and pleasure,
Despair and hope,
Melancholy and gaiety
Clamour and silence
Solitude and companionship
Every moment of life is liked,
Held precious and invaluable.
Yet a piquant feeling
Of inactivity and vapidity
Fidgets, itches and incites a wish—
Wish to get up
Leave the bed
To be ambulant,
Revitalize the nerves
For breaking again
Arduous rocks of life.

But a fragile heart
With irregular pulses,
Eyes with feeble sight
And
Body with flaccid muscles
Clip the wings of this wish,
Cramp the style
And leave "compromise"
The only option.

The beats of a broken clock
The pulses of a fragile heart,
Unfold nonchalance of fugitive time
Reveal inequity of limited life.

World: an intricate oddity per se
Time and life its crossword
Man, its zealous solver,
Before conjuring any solution
Turns unqualified,
And dropped out!
Sense of nostalgia enveloping thoughts
His lips seem to whisper—
Afsoos Duniya Kahsina Lug Samsaar Sethi . . .

Me And I

Engrossed in temporal affairs
Concerned about fame and name,
I missed a rendezvous with Me
Ah, I missed!

It was simply touch of nature
Or a dessert after starving wait,
That somehow Me had descended into
my world
Had just knocked my door
Tried to strike a chord somewhere
And create ripples of perpetual calm.

But due to noisy gibberish of heart
and cold blood inside,
I reacted passively.
I ignored the knock
didn't jump out of joy
or
Sang loud salutations.

Me came again, but this time
I was fast asleep
Wandering in dreams,
building utopia.

Even as stray dogs howled
leaves rustled
And doors, windows creaked,
I but couldn't open starry-eyes.
Eventually Me left,
Left perhaps for good
Never to return into my being.

Alas, I couldn't be me
though Me could have been I!

A Companion

Many a thought, many a vista
it swallows silently.
Everyday a new story,
a new glimmer, a new irony
I dump in it.
And I wonder,
how patiently it endures
the brunt of my whimsicality!

The paper load of disposable words
some sweet, some sour,
some realities, some imaginings
I rive and throw away in it
rather nonchalantly.

The rhapsody of songs
the monotony of dreams
the cacophony of wishes,
all in black and white,
it grins and bears.

I know it aspires
to do away with me,
but can't.
Why?
It beats me!

Each morn it is emptied,
given a dust
and placed back under my table
to die in harness sneeringly.
Each morn my reticent feelings
are disposed off,
my mind is littered out
on the street waste,
making to a happy hunting ground!
And all this and everything
here below gets cast off
and heaped in this sole companion,
my dusty coloured dustbin.

Oscillations

In betwixt day and night
autumn and Spring,
A moment occurs
when the heart bursts
like a cloud
due to thunder of memories.

Key of nostalgia
breaks the lock,
Reopens old chambers
old sores,
as experience pricks
and
bitterness bleeds.

Scattered files of
unknown bruises
unknown crimes
stir emotions.

Scars of innocence
residing beneath
every broken fragment,
infuriate a twinge
invoke a tear.

Dark Room

Harbouring the images
Developing the pictures
Just out of dark thoughts.

The darkling faces in silhouette,
Concentric rings of hope
Revolve round till
Vanishing at dead end.

A small streak of light
mars the whole creation,
exposes hollowness of make-believe.

Ideas become foggy
Imaginations remain imaginings!
Superficial solutions of slush
never blend with pure water
to create a perpetual bond.

Fixers fail to fix them together
on the glossy paper of life.

In the dead dark corner
of dark room,
Realities suffocate and darkle
as blackness never gleams outside.

Lame Time

Through the corridors of time
when every moment dissipated,
all doors to vast expanse
Of experience opened.
Dulcet voices disclosed tales
of committed linnets and mock-birds,
of Cupid and Caliban.
Colours revealed discrepancy
white here, black there,
Red the Scaffold, golden the Crown.
Beaming light pierced across,
Ugliness blemished beauty
And corporeal outclassed ethereal.

Shrieks, shrills;
tears, torments;
smiles, sighs;
joys, jitters—
A slice of life
purported a wondrous mosaic.

Many years on, but Time
seems congealed,
words and deeds frozen.
Seeds never sprouted
and flowers never bloomed.
In the cosmos, a midget swung
dateless far and wide.
In an errand of mercy
with no purlieus,
it drifted away
escaping from the hold of account.

Today fetterless but aimless
it crumbles under
the piles of shame,
the heaps of sin
and
the beats of Lame Time.

Realities

If it is Wound
Blood will bleed;

If it is Eye
Tears will trickle;

If it is Heart
Throbs will sink;

If it is Conscience
Facts will prick.

In the market of voices,
silence will fade.

Howling matters
but
Realities seldom change.

Thank You, God!

A small opening
when doors are closed.
A streak of light
when darkness has invaded.

The Divine Help
The Divine Hand,
behind the veils
beneath the skies,
Obliterates past regrets
Inscribes avid future.

The crooked line of Fate
straightens its course.
Static stars start stalking,
Weakest hopes turn into
firm convictions
and
Distant aims become realities.

God, The Great Giver
Listens sighs, supplications
of those baulked in despair.
Dispatches a "Relief Package"
beautifully decorated with
tags of pure dreams,
ribbons of noble desires
plus
a range of sincere compliments
exuding fragrance of well-wishing.
Invisible Souls
Invisible Lips,
Convey the message
Compose the occasion.

Surely, laughter and tears
bliss and infelicity
are in His Hands.
There is none like unto Him
There is no god but He.
Thank God, God does care!

Trade of Relations

A flower swallowed by bud,
A nest
marauded by dwellers,
A garden
Withered by leaves.
Can thee imagine?

Incoherence of minds
malaise of hearts
false affection
selfish sympathy
in conjunction,
under one sky.
Can thee imagine?

Eyes nonchalant
towards sight.
Entangled in cocoons
bonds of love
displaying apathy,
Blood turning thin.
Can thee imagine?

Self and Self
I and I,
Give and take
Interest and loss
Trade of relations,
Diminishing sincerity.
Can thee imagine?

Yea, here!
Where apple of eye
at times
is an eyesore.
Narrow outlets,
narrow inlets.
Choked sentiments
estranged affinities—all galore,
all gamble.

A Flight

These white hands of mine
knit up prolonged twilights
upon my closed eyes.

My tongue was lost and dumb,
and had forgotten to sing
the very old songs
once sung.

But the light of candle lamp
lit up my room.

It was the soothing light,
the yellowish against drizzly dusk.

And the most melodious solitude
was just fascinating.

The solitude dangled
before the flickers of candle,
and settled the medley
of my mind
to a beautiful calmness,
like the sea responding
to the melody of moon magic.

The timeless time
crept in me as my soul,
like aura of sun
in brilliant hues,
through the ozone holes
in dusky poles.

Somewhere,
in midst of this moment
I missed somebody:
Yes, my own self!

Utopia

Under the sun
A small place,
Somewhere . . .
Peace of mind
Tranquility of heart
and
Satisfaction of soul,
Let thou pursue.

Leaving behind
Everything
Every possession
Every creature comfort
and
Even every akinship,
Let thou flee.

Where superficiality
Sham of relations
Selfishness
Are unfamiliar traits.

Where purity of hearts
Coherence of words and deeds
Honesty of attitudes
Fills thy existence.

Where complaisance
compassion
composure
Are thy treasures.

Somewhere . . .
Where love begets love
Good reciprocates,
Let thou seek.

Somewhere . . . .
a small corner
a small space,
Neither a mansion
Nor any coffers
Let thou create.

Far from crowd
Far from impostors
Far from obscure faces.

Somewhere . . .
In a hush of silence
Let thou adorn
They own world,

Thy own nest
With the straws of honesty,
With the twigs of sincerity.

Somewhere thy unreached abode
lies unaltered.

A Silver Lining

When nature stops
weeping for gladness,
Clouds move
firmament gets clear
brightness radiates,
Then
Daffodils in garden
blush with ease,
Sparrows twitter
Pigeons coo
and
Splash of mirth
daubs thy heart.

Uncalled for optimism
unknown hopes,
Like innocent buds
bloom smiles.

Soul aches
heart soothes,
Reason baffles
impulse handles—
Thine elevation
Thine flight of joy.

An insatiable satisfaction
A wandering wish
Lingers on
only so long as
A silver lining
accompanied with clouds
appears again
and
takes the bloom off!

A Wanton Fury

To chop logic into pieces
and
roast it on smouldering fire,
I want to kill Sanity.
Am I allowed?

To thrash Ideals down
and
vandalize the temples of Passion,
I want to go berserk.
Am I allowed?

To sleep over the Pathos
and
benumb the senses to Apathy,
I want to be stolid.
Am I allowed?

To mingle fragrance of Flowers
and
pungent breath of Cedars,
I want to be brute.
Am I allowed?

To live in snug of Oblivion
and
move deep into crevices of Earth
I want to crawl incognito.
Am I allowed?

To stare at the face of Speech
and
listen to the moaning of Silence,
I want to be deaf-mute.
Am I allowed?

To close the clumsy Eyes
and
blink over the searing Realities,
I want to play damn fool.
Am I allowed?

To bequeath the tricky Dreams
and
scrape the quarry Images,
I want to enjoy nightmares.
Am I allowed?

To shut up the bad Mouth
and
spit out the mad Heart,
I want to sing a swan-song.
Am I allowed?

Antidote

Bitten, bruised by a bait
He needed it
for a living.

Mauled, smeared by a bait
He needs it
for he is dying.

The Antidote to his
death:
The Death of death.

Bear

Held in cosy arms
Kissed by soft lips
Caressed by velvety hands
Tight in warm embrace
he aint the bear,
Teddy, he is.

Mauled by gnawing teeth
Bruised by brute force
Lacerated by merciless claws
He is the bear,
bugbear, he is.

Yet man needs to bear both.

But Perhaps

The impulses
Throbs of thy dudgeon
Pangs of conscience
Perhaps I can hear;
Iniquitous attitude
Injustice on thy part
For an unknown crime
Perhaps I can realise;
Depth of bitterness
Thine indignation
Against all
Perhaps I can gauge;
Tears of torment
Tornado of aversion
In thine eyes
Perhaps I can see;
Hurt psyche
Ragged sentiments
Pricking thou inly
Perhaps I can sense.
But perhaps,
Shackles on reason
Thy handcuffs
I can't break,

I really can't.
Forlorn myself
Striving for survival,
I can only be
A mute spectator.
I can't even shout,
I can't even cry.
But perhaps
I can shut my eyes
Kill my conscience
And
Leave thou groaning
For all the time.

Sorry historians,
I'm helpless.
History is always
a brute goddess.

Her Soul

Dreamt he had
Of her charms
Of her beauty
Of her approval.

Died he unheard
Of her indifference
Of her spurn
Of her reprimand.

Searching her soul
He continues to live,
Yet his soul dead.

A Far Cry

While over the horizons
Beyond limits of zenith,
Upon the clouds
Winds dangled me in ecstasy,
My wings suddenly ruffled with
The dust storm in the air.

I started wavering, lying low
Fearing a fall,
A terrible fall.

I gave up my flight
Settled below down just there
On a small piece of land.

The eerie silence around
Was dead dark there
And
So were the days and nights.

Sun seldom shoved past my abode
And moon never blinked at my state.

Each moment brought
A whiff of vexation

A whimper of vagueness,
Until once I clipped
My weak wings forever.

Relieved of the burden
I had been dragging for long,
I was no more a birdie
No more even a bird fancier.

But
I was what I'm now
A blithe and blest earthling,
Accepting whatever I'm given
Returning whatever I'm receiving.

And this piece of land now,
Its inhabitants,
Its tragedies,
Its pleasures,
And I:
All live in consonance
All breathe in reconciliation.

All is set in order
God above, Heavens above
I below, my land below,
Very below the very above,
And
Very far, very farther.

A Scream

A scream that falls,
ripping open the sky.

A scream that takes flight,
lifting the sea.

A scream that collides
with itself,
like the rocks licking fire.

A scream that makes
a bird burst out in laughter.

A scream that prompts
demons of thirst to lurk.

A scream that awakens
the nocturnal delight.

A scream that succours
death to take respite
on cold carpets of blood
like an atrocious sadist.

A scream that is
only mine,
just mine
and
has remained unchanged
since times immemorial.

Fidelity

Abode of my dreams
with the sun on the walls,
carries its elegance
as of a seraphic touch.

Holds the depth of the sea,
the charisma of the rainbow.

A songbrid grows out of mist,
its sweet note medleys
with the trance of my soul.

I am swallowed up in clouds,
gliding gleefully.

Reach out your hand
Search me out,
Listlessly lost
I am.

My thoughts fluttering in vague
My instincts fleeting unknown.

Hold me back,
don't let go
my sweet wilderness.

Making me a whole
grasping a moment
beyond bondages.

Faithfully I stand, My Lord.

Another Dark Night

In the dead of night,
in the awesome ambience
when the streets were deserted
and
the hush of silence
was stirred by
sighing of wind,
warbling of crickets,
intermittent howling
of stray dogs,
Not far from the city
someone was awake
preparing to die
for those who were in slumber.

As the monsters of death approached,
every breath of his became precious
and every pulse irretrievable.

Caught in a black hole,
his memory flipped:

The face of his caring mother
his beloved better-half
and his innocent children
sparked like a lightening
in the enveloping darkness.

Tears welled up in his eyes,
his heart sank in nostalgia
and like the crack of doom
words slipped unwittingly
from his lips.

He cried, in wilderness:
Help, Help . . . .

But alas!
No response to his swan-song.

The rattle of bullets,
the bang of mortar shells
buried him forever
under the heap of oblivion.

Yet another slave soul,
lived and died.

Yet another drop of blood,
smearing the annals of history.

Yet another evanescent cry,
rending the air of apathy.

Yet another dark night passed by,
as the violent cacophony continues.

Stormy Lethe

Flowing through the hearts
Eroding the barriers
Sliding into every mind,
The storm of Lethe
overtook all.

Eighty thousand souls
bulk of blood
pathetic cries
innocent tears,
It washed away . . .
washed abruptly!

Nothing has happened
nothing will happen.
Dale is now 'smiling'
Gardens are 'blooming'
and
Chinars are 'rejoicing'.

Which Sacrifice?!
Whose Death?!
Where is the Caravan?!
Where is 'Ameer'?!
Where is Track?!
Where is Torch?!

Nothing was there
nothing will be.
Inconstant moods
Inscrutably unpredictable,
Infirm memory—
Unfold not tantrums
but
indelible traits.

Swim with the Lethe,
Sell down the Vitasta.
Follow waves,
Forget graves
Forget evermore!

The Waterloo

Far from the ocean of crowd
when torrential tides
wreaked havoc with the present and
past was swept away into oblivion;

When historian was shocked
and felt an odd twinge
while committing to the immortal papers
the every discernible event
of every unalterable passing minute;

When apes donned the apparel of Kings,
palaces were profaned,
human decorum effaced;

When ship was bogged down by turmoil
a few callous sailors proved spectators
and flagstaff eventually broke;

When deceased were in throes
graveyards became invisible,
marauded home was out of mind;

When wounds not yet healed
were squeezed,
and every trickling drop of blood
gradually clotted
on a dead faint conscience.

I was somewhere,
Somewhere in unknown suspense
in forced hibernation.
Evading the realities
trying to be just deaf mute.
But
I know I wasn't all asleep.
My eyes were open,
my heart was pulsating
and
I closely witnessed
the barbaric murder:
the Waterloo of Chequered History!

Reminder

Overflowing roads
Jam packed vehicles
Busy markets
Decorated restaurants
Glittering dresses
Bright and swanky faces
Music rending the air
Aroma of a freshly prepared
cuisine going by.

All in a hurry.
Working in tandem,
Only one motive in mind—
Enjoy and have fun.

Yes, a right to have
a gala time,
for it is Eid day.

No matter the poor widow
needs to beg.

No one to console the father
whose tears have gone dry
for his lone and missing son.

The daughter whose honour
stays in tatters.

The martyr whose voice
remains stifled.

The poor, the needy, all forgotten.

In despair and agony,
now unheard and unsung
in oblivion.

Was it a dream
that is forgotten now?!
Or we have forgotten
that we forget?!

Our idols smashed to smithereens.
Our icons turned turn-coats.

A nation sans heroes.
A nation sans leaders.
A nation sans conscience.

A nation that has lost its identity.
A nation that had long been
sold before in paper.
Now sold forever,
even in dreams!

Unknown Voice

Adieu my mother, adieu!
Tear not your hair.
Dead I am not.
Around your lap,
Always will I be
Invisible, listening to
Those sweet songs
Which you had
Knit for my knot!

Adieu my father, adieu!
Though on last journey
I am
But first passenger
I am not.
O, father of martyr
Don't stagger
Alive I am,
Alive I will be!

Adieu my sisters, adieu!
Don't recall me
In hisses and sobs,
Back will I be
In your dreams
In your thoughts
To see you
In bridal apparel
With henna hands!

Adieu my friends, adieu!
Wipe out scalding tears,
Miss you can't me
For memories of
Shared moments
Will bind me
Close to you
To your hearts
Always!

Adieus and Adieus forever!

Return Of Phoenix

Last frozen night
when gloom hung in the air
like a pestilent cloud,
not a whiff of air
not a branch stirred.

But the wings of a dream
fluttered over the dreamscape
in mine part of mouthful sky.

In the eerie silence of
leafless trees,
a hovering echoed like
a music from the lute.

A sudden waft of air
hissed past my face,
conveying a message of its own.

Something inside me cringed
as under the spell of
shimmering light
from a magic lantern,
I saw world in my eyes

with a frozen pain,
a fractured agony.

Mermaids were lulling fiery songs
and
bleeding roses were gasping.

The cramped roll of fate
had snatched so much . . . .
the bright faces, the young souls
the vitality, the virility
the peace, the tranquility
the honour, the dignity.

Yet, a dulcet voice
from Happy Isles
deciphered the obscure secret,
delivered the glad tidings.
The Phoenix had come!

To divulge that dreams slip in,
as life flows on anyhow.

What if dead babies are
fished out from drains,
sisters have gone astray,
brothers are loitering . . . .
the wolves go on living,
fatter and merrier
they grow endlessly.

What if orphans become criminals,
widows start begging,
bullets boomerang . . . .
the black hearted black men
with bagfuls of black money
continue to dabble in sins,
the blackest ever.
Adversity withers, prosperity blooms.

What if I kill you
and you kill everybody;

What if drones and moths
sting the innocence;

What if you worship the rising sun
and chase the fugitive sunshine;

What if rivers are stagnated
and hills stand naked
because of foul deeds?

Any moment now, any day now
you'll be taken in for repairs
the Phoenix told me.

Morbid brains, malicious hearts
would be overhauled.

And a small band of animals
will stride out upon the earth,
upright, firm and strong,
avid to weave a dream . . . .

To see a stream of consciousness
awaking conscience from
waking slumber
and
making you humans humane.

None leaves for good.
Like Phoenix, all come back
in different shadows.

To weep a bit again,
to smile a little again,
to live a while again and
to weave a dream
again and yet again.

Come, let's weave a dream,
Aow Ki Koi Khwaab Bunein . . . .

All Blood, No Snow

When the long night
melted into nothingness,
the dim twinkling of stars vanished.

Alien dust wiped out
all the foot prints
and drowned all lamps in fog.

Time like fortune was unfriendly
and the face of dawn scarred
like wintry sun that
peeped through the mute hills,
as clouds had gone
into blank vacuum of imagination.

The chilly breeze
knocked at every door
saying words without meaning.

All doors were closed,
bolted inside.
All ears were blocked with cobwebs,
lips sealed and hearts pierced.

Just yesterday, the man was butchered
outside on the street.
His intestines were scattered
around his corpse.
He lay there for long
untouched, unclaimed
even as stray dogs licked his blood.

Just yesterday, the apple of eye
was killed in a crowded market.
He had gone to fetch some milk.
Milk he never got,
back he never returned.
Everlasting tears, he gifted to his mother.

Just yesterday, numerous coffins
reached to the graveyard,
numerous cries went in the air
like pebbles sinking
noiselessly in the sand.

Just yesterday, so many sisters' hope
so many mothers' joy,
so many sons,
so many youthful faces,
so many buds, so many flowers
so many fragrances, so many yearnings . . . .
all got buried
deep down into the oblivion.

Yes, we have learned to live
with death
but what lies behind escapes us all.

It is our dreams!

Dreams of voices that are silenced,
of doors that wait to be opened.

Dreams for whom we gave our life,
we gave our everything.

Dreams which carry with them
the beauty of our tears,
the treasure of our blood.

Dreams which taste no roses, no snow
but blood, only blood.

Dreams which hide all tragedies
beneath their wings
and soar above all sufferings.

Dreams which whisper to us:
Chend Roz Aur Meri Jaan!
Fakht Chend Hi Roz . . .
'Lets endure a little longer
for we may have to endure today
but not forever.'

Dreams which invoke morning breeze
to bring some words, some songs
or even an elegy that would
steer the forgetful memory
out of the Lethe.

Dreams which saw dreams
laced in blood
and handed them unfilled
to their dreamers.

Just yesterday, the transition
took place.

We, sullen and wry,
crawled to hop over it
as we have been crawling for years.

We saw our bloody dreams
sliced into moments,
flinging into symbol of time.

We saw our bloody dreams
drifting aimlessly like autumn leaves,
drenching in the dust of time.

We saw our bloody dreams
gasping as we continue to die,
and die very cheap.

We saw our bloody dreams
dripping blood from festering visions
of dead yesterdays
and
unborn tomorrows.
We saw it, and saw it all,
just silently, just helplessly.
We left certain things unsaid,
we left certain things unheard.
We left an unopened window
on the unmade world,
on the unborn hopes,
on the unfulfilled dreams,
as the over-blown millennium
sneaked in unbidden.

Seesaw

This dread,
this dance . . . .

This glee,
this gloom . . . .

Vicious circles
and
their tentacles.

I glide with them
all in me . . . .

I am happy,
I am sad.

Future of The Past

In the mist of despair
when not to speak of a thousand suns,
even a solitary one was eclipsed,
drowned into gloom.

It was when moon never existed
and
stars were absolutely unknown.

It was when clouds of irony,
incinerated every hope,
and
ashes of reality were charred.

Agony, anarchy and annihilation
had seeped deep into
every bit of matter.

Time was agile
and waiting in the wings.

Lo! it slipped out,
froze far and farther away,
never to return.

It left us behind
alone and hapless,
to writhe in past,
to decay in nothingness.

Empty, void and dark,
no memorable moments to recollect,
unknowingly we clinged
to vacuous past
as even Past passed-by stealthily.

Yes!
illusions, mirages
we watered
and
reaped nothing in return.

Dancing oceans
hidden in our chests,

Crystal streams shimmering
in our hearts,

Ponds of moon shining
in our sunken eyes,

Flurry of waves thumping
in our beleaguered souls,

We just dreamed . . . . .
Dreamed in vanity, we?!

We reared nothing
but
the misplaced hopes,
the misread realities,
the misplayed notions,
and
held back the empty past,
choking its veins to death:

It was painful, pathetic
but a pious fraud
with no one
but ourselves
as Future vainly tried
to wriggle out
from the shackles of past.

Motherly Verse

Weakling, fledgling
lazy and fool,
she calls me often
as I mismanage chores.

A grimace on face
eyes glowing with anger,
she rebukes me often
as I mistime instructions.

Fretting and fuming,
she curses her own training,
fears an 'Incompetent Teacher'
she'll be called
for her daughter
can't excel as a 'Virtuous Woman'.

But no, dear Mama, no!
Keep cool, rest assured!

Food I will cook
Dishes I will wash
Rooms I will sweep
Floors I will mop
Clothes I will iron

Guests I will serve
and above all
fain everything I will endure
ala conventional lady,
in coherence with your lessons
carrying conviction.

Woman is born to suffer:
you often say.

She treads different roads.
Meets saints and sinners.
Laughs with the winners.

Weeps for the losers.
Lives for others.
Dies for herself.

Assimilating much,
asserting little
she learns, unlearns and relearns
many a truth.

From a cry-baby
to
a story-telling granny,
she remains a lady in obeisance.

The odyssey of life leads her on,
on and on . . .

The dimples vanish,
the wrinkles visit.
She remains unchanged.

The mirth of childhood,
halcyon of youth,
autumn of old age.
She remains unchanged.

Yes, dear Mama,
I can't dare to be
an Iconoclast!

A Murmur Within

The earth was same
and
so was the sky above.

Gusts of wind
permeated through
the same crevices
of small walls
into that room,
where everything was
just lying still
as it was.

Only a candle,
a few papers
and
a pen,
among all other lifeless things
were singing the
same old song.

Candle flickered hopes
papers turned nostalgic, and
pen spilled some scalding tears.

The old story was
yet incomplete,
still inconclusive.

From the year dot
the end seemed obscure,
and so was it today.

Nothing had changed
except the shattered anima
of the battered soul
haunting that room.

Its charisma gone,
its appeal lost,
its black veil of puritanism
was lying abandoned
in the cupboard
of blighted exhibitionism.

Among new blues, new pinks
new tawdry colours,
the forsaken black
craved for resurrection,
calling unknown Saviour
who is just somewhere nigh.

But
the bathos was
the same outstayed wait,
exhausting the exuberance
of the candle,
paper and pen.

Winters Voice

Those long dark, cold nights
and dry chilly days.
Long queues around and
a mad rush for anything available.

As we grope in the dark,
confused as ever,
to welcome him with unease,
discomfort and melancholy.

An anathema to the poor and sick,
portending a gala time for elite.

As he starts his sojourn.
come miseries galore.
Spiraling prices, power cuts,
frozen taps, scarce commodities
and chaotic roads.

Problems, problems all the way,
for those who don't forget
the New Year in their dreams.

No, they don't ever!
They fail to remember it actually.

Hey, Hello! Happy New Year.
I am from the RANGEEN PALACE.
We are having a nice dinner party,
and an 'exclusively for couples
ball dance tonight'.
Happy New Year to you too . . .
The phone snapped.

Inside a departmental store,
I saw guys and gals
buying new year cards, souvenirs,
'talking hearts', and
all that which matters to the
love-sick and love-stupid.

Some making hush-hush buzz calls,
giggling, smiling,
oblivious of
their future and of me.

One among them hissing . . .
Hello! *Hello-Farmayish*,
Can you play *Kuch Kuch Hota Hai?*

Screeching to an abrupt halt
I see a *Marvati Car*,
the occupants in tight jeans,

spotting Raybans.
With contemptuous eyes, they,
the neo-riche,
scan the Sunday market,
Where teeming crowds
look for cheaper clothes
to save themselves from
the frozen turbulence.
Yaar, yeh second-hand maal hai!
Let's go to the Warehouse—they fret.

I board a bus,
plying through the
narrow roads of Srinagar,
as if traversing the clogged
arteries of its bruised heart.

The bus overflowing with passengers,
jostling, sneering, arguing,
and hoping that winter is dry
for otherwise they'll be out of work.

A prayer that is poison
to the ears of eco-freaks,
for they want us to see
mountains yelling with snow
and
rivers barking with water.
After all, *Power Ka Sawaal hai*!

As I went down the bus
a hundred people crossing the road,
accompanying the coffin to graveyard,
their faces sullen and wry,
I asked who was he?
'He was an oldie,
suffering from asthma.
Winter took toll of him'.
Yet another quipped—
'*Wakht Aosus Wotmut*'.

In a daily paper I read
a dozen obit about *Rasm-e-Chahrum*
Unnerved, disturbed and panicky,
I yearned for a place
where I could hide sorrily.

I managed a place in the
cosy *Hammam* of a mosque,
where young and old were
chatting and gossiping,
talking all but Allah.

Exasperated, I left straight
for the airport.
Caught in crossfire, I however
missed the flight and
returned back with a heavy heart.

I'm waiting for the flight,
fervently longing to leave,
for my presence here
except to a minuscule elite,
is agonizing.

How I wish never to visit
this place ever again!

Yes, I am Winter of Kashmir.

Keep Going

Thunder after a shower
Darkness after light
Coffins and cradles
Ruins and dwellings
I watched by and went on.

Thorns pricked,
my feet bled
and left the crimson foot prints.

I looked not around,
turned nor hear
as fate ridiculed me at the back.

Chasing the fugitive sunshine,
looking for shadows,
I couldn't catch a fly-by-night.

I fell down,
broke myself.

But
it was the first and last fall,
the first and last midsummer madness.

Crawling like a dead-duck,
gathering shattered pieces,
stood I straight somehow again,
walked patiently
and faced the world.

Even as my fragile boats
capsized in tempest,
A bridge of sorts I still
persist to build
between
me and life.

Do's and Don'ts

They are thine intimate associates
clinging to thou every time,
Making thy life a scathing experience.

An odious shadow they form
which chases thee,
as if thou are a fugitive culprit.

A zone of limitation they mark
beyond which thou can't transgress,
thy steps circumscribed become.

Believed strongly it is that
a constant fumigation with these
makes thy brain 'fool proof',
pathogens of folly hardly infect!

Ergo a sign-board gets hanged
around thine neck.

Wherever thou go
and
whatever thou do,
it alarms thee:

"Don't put a foot wrong
follow the laid 'norms',
since thou are a fledgling
still an insensible chap".

A Mirage

In the desert of trials
where drought of dreams
had played havoc,
A caravan of strangers
passed by.

Camping for a while,
they tilled the barren soil.

Hopes they sow
and
wishes they watered.

An oasis
it seemed they created,
for a different language they spoke.

But lo!
A whirlwind stormed the desert,
everything was rooted out.

Hopes withered again into wounds
and
Wishes blew down by pangs.

Strangers left,
caravan changed its course,
Desert was deserted.

Only a mirage remained . . .

Mirage of camaraderie.
It snatched all dreams
that the specious morn unseen
had once instilled
in the stolid gale.

Ah, a betrayal
went unnoticed
in the silent show!

Broken Idols

Yesterday's autumn wind has
blown them all.
Scattered hither and yon,
every broken fragment of theirs
displays a false glitter still.

Yes, my dear, they never shined.
It was just your naivety
that guided you into sandstorms,
that wounded your soul.

Ignorance, dear, just ignorance
blinded you,
you took Idols as Angels!
And adulated them to the hilt,
little knowing that crags never cry.

The tallest idol at Tokyo
is yet intact.
Even the Statue of Liberty
still stands high in the air.
Its fumeless flambeau mocking
all the slaves of the world.

But
your small, inconspicuous idols
have fallen on evil times.

Smashed and razed to the ground,
they tell you nothing . . . .
Nothing about the next moment,
the next day, the next summer.

The solitary ringdove there
fails to vent the vagaries of autumn.
Who knows when she will coo
in a feel-good tone,
announcing the presence of
a pie in the sky.

Who knows when a wintry sun
that has gone into hiding
behind the mountains,
will come out and
disperse the rays of hope.

Who knows when snow will melt down
the fire of burning earth
and fill up its crevices
with a sheeny trust
that'll bury the broken idols
deep into the oblivion . . .
never to be traced,
never to be recreated.

They say cloning is possible.
But tell you what,
Idols shouldn't be cloned.
Never!

Their mysterious appeal,
their surreal charisma
its all ephemeral.

They speak the same language—the Greek,
and dwell in the same haunted lane.

Remember, what Allama told you a long ago:
Boutu Sai Tuj ko Umeday
Khuda Sai Naumeede!—
You are hopeful of Idols
but not God!

And its apostasy to worship idols,
you heard in a homily
the other day.

The idols too heard it
and laughed at you
in as proud as Lucifer's style.

In the voice of Khayyam,
they ridiculed:
'O fool, we've done your credit
in this world much wrong,
we've drowned your glory in a shallow cup
And sold your reputation for a song'.

You stand bewildered,
consoling yourself with alibis.

Ghalib sees through your heart
and wavers to whisper:
'Imaan Tujay Rokai Hai
Jo Kheechai Hai Tujay kufr'—
Faith stops you
from being faithless.

Not near the Kaaba,
neither in the Church,
but you reside amidst
blurry shadows of broken idols
In the temple of your heart . . .
dilemmatic as ever
erratic as always.

Nonetheless, fallen from grace
the idols have.

It needed no iconoclast
but idols themselves.

Nonchalance

"Save me, Save me"!
were his only words.

Lying on the wrecked stretcher
Fighting with death,
His deep wounds bled.

Fingers trembled,
Voice choked
And
Tears slowly trickled.

"Save me, Save me"!
were his only words.

Moved by his pathetic pain
I called on
Champions of treatment
Specialists of world
Stalwarts of humanity:
UNO, OIC, Red Cross, Amnesty.

I blubbered and beseeched,
Begged his survival and nothing else.

They excused and avoided,
They nodded and stammered—
"No, N-o, cha-chance a-at-a-ll"

Dream Portrait

A hanging picture on my wall;
A tattered image of passing soul
Not a calendar
But
the portrait of a frozen Dream.

It looks so shabby; immensely awful.
Garlanded by cobwebs
dust wraps it.

The unsightliness lingers,
but the moments of pain seem to wane.
I remember the melancholy strain,
of sweet music and
lost loves in days long past.
All stands crystallized in my memory.

The smell and warmth of lineage,
I am part of it,
a strand in the tapestry of time;
Intertwined with everything
that happened to portrait.

I stand here, in front of it;
I am forever changed,
Never to be same,
So is it!

Occasionally, a wave knocked
around in our peaceful drift,
an unexpected thunderstorm
reacquaints us.

Reassured, we sail to bigger islands,
but in separate directions.
A bitter experience binds closer.

Time brings change in us;
A fissure glides
dream away, slowly . . . .
now stuck up in a deadwood frame.

Today I stare it,
peep into its unpredictable contours;
mock its false form
and
weep at its emptiness.

People die for dreams;
water them with their
tears and blood.
But dreams still die!
Revolutions are aborted.

I find this revelation sad
yet shed no tear;
Rather I dance in the
dusty ruins of my dream,
drink from its dropped wounds,
and ridicule my silly creation.

I laugh at the portrait, tragically.

Still . . . . I hear the echoes
footsteps fading in the shadows;
clearly telling me not to be ruthless.

Yet here I sit . . .
Touching the dream portrait,
wiping out dust from it . . . .
My faults, emphasized.
My hands on it . . . . my hands are its own,
my face is its face . . . .
it reflects my reflection!

We keep our tombs full of same memories,
locked with the same obstinate determination.
We are strangers, distanced forever
living in different worlds now;
yet I know we think about each other . . . . .
Sometimes,
unknowingly,
And prevent tears to trickle down.
Time flits, years pass by;
dust settles on both of us
Me and the portrait.

My Songs

No flute in the wind I am,
Yet singing my own songs.

The beat of drums,
the wrestling wind,
the rustling grass,
the gentle breeze—
synchronize all
with my unspoken syllables.

Nightingales, cuckoos,
all and sundry
hover in the wind,
shadowing me,
listening to my tuneless symphony.

They adore me!
For no one ever sang for them.

The moist tears
carry their unintelligible words,
the somber thoughts
espouse their existence
like writing
an indelible language on an olive branch.

Scented by memories
adorned by warmth,
pulled by the moon
carried by the sun
and
lured by the stars
They bury all my notes.

To remember them for ever,
for I rarely revere them.

A Fresh Verve

I am soaring over
untouched domain.
I am soaring over
unmatched dreams.

The wind whipping in my face
as I fly
over intangible terrains.

The beauty is bizarre!

The rising sun
peeps over the summit.

Colours of hope and harmony
weave a backdrop
for a new-fangled flight,
against stony
hate and hauteur
sham and sadness.

The dives swirl me,
defy my fears.

I see skies hugging me.

My dreamscape welcomes me
with a surprising spectacle
of furtive
but genuine vows.

The lodestar suavely
enlightens my blindness.

I see my dream
with naked eye.

The fairy dromedaries
sand my faith in miracles.

The apogee of jubilation
kisses my loneliness.
My vision drools over
the longevity of truth.

I scoff at my past,
soaring over the
beauty of life
and
stuffing the ugliness
forever in ruins.

A Pyrrhic Victory

Rattling guns, roaring missiles
Bomb sprinkled figures
On the frozen ground,
a bloody shroud of a child.
Unsung!

Congealed looks
vacant souls,
Blood-spattered armor,
gore slicked bodies
guns wailing over mutilated organs.
Is this all what we aspired for?

Silence reigns
mourning beneath the sun,
Don't take me as chicken hearted.
For the tears I shed are yours.
Where should I begin
to reveal the heart full of burden?

Where is the victory we were promised?
For your angst-ridden youth,
your snatched dreams
and the fates that brought to this war.
It's only tragedy I find!

Sleep in peace ye dead of winter
and pray peace is what I find,
as the cold winds keep to my back
and I leave you all behind.

Silent Talk

The assured love
for my dead,
has not washed away.

Today I forge a link
with them,
visit their hearth
and shower flowers
on their graves.

They ask about life,
they enquire about others.

I feign to give no answer
but listen to them endlessly.

A long silence follows.

They watch me mute.
I stare them.

The stony tombs
and a few mortal narcissus,
the stray dogs
and a few speckled carcasses—
something around
is transpiring.

My dead are still alive

But . . .

I seem to be dead!

Déjà Vu

I voyaged to the ocean today
in order to trail the sun . . .

I built a citadel made of sand
when the tide was out,
in order to style my symphony.

I left it there for the others
and it was finally brushed away.

I went to go surf
when the surge was in,
in order to ride the wave where it takes me.
And I crashed upon the beach
in a wheezing muddle.

When I looked up to the deep,
it was as the sun were
sneering me.

I stumped my tongue
out in revulsion,
and it got blazed.

I voyaged to the ocean today
in order to trail the sun . . .
the fugitive sun,

And
I left only with
a pitcher for my silence,
a pail for my regret . . .

Radio Kashmir

Dark nights alone
yet we dream together.
Our vision not a fluke,
No ghost in the snow

Finding her. Can we?
Her touch
that shall enliven.
Her presence
that shall remit the
loneliness.

I had heard
She will!
Radio Kashmir
said—she loves us all.
Loves *Raheem*, loves *Raina*
yet we don't yearn for her now.

Passions cool
blood trickles
houses smoke
As we drift, alone.
Our vision
a mirage in the desert.

Darker nights,
now we dream alone
trying to avoid sleep.
Waking undesirous
moving into oblivion.

Radio Kashmir
really sings. So
they say.

Darkest nights now our fate
and we stop
even dreaming alone!

A Swan song

An orange coloured moon
drips into my palms,
just a little late.

And it's the last
silver of the moon that cuts
through my blood.

It doesn't see the aura
it once held in me.
Jaded, we are both!

An empty
ocean tide traveled by
a few angels in pain,
rises to fall
and falls to rise.

I am at shore
holding moon in levity,
in disguised peace.

My eyes move inarticulate,
wearied by affectation.

Howls of passion
pass into whimper.

The punctured sky
picks my swan-song
without mouthing a whisper,
or shedding a tear.

I too am
unswayed,
unmoved.

Anonymity

Blindly anonymous,
I couldn't find words
that could express me.

Downtown middle class mentality,
nothing really remarkable
I have got!

The words
that demand and
crave attention,
stagger to reason.

A dilemma,
out of the emotional miasma.

A sheer absurdity
spiced with
helplessness at the heart.

Frazzled and downcast,
I cease to ask for
some blonde hash
some bogus antics.

I refuse to buy
humiliation.

Anonymity became anonymous.

A Dilemma

In thoughts of anguish
Fused I am momentarily
into scenes
when I couldn't find
a hope to hang on.

It won't be the same,
I knew.

I continued
my search for words.

Fears faded slowly.

Today I want heaven
and I want it in shipshape!
And if I don't get to it,
doesn't matter.
It just doesn't matter

It won't be the same,
I know.

Today I want stars to
drive me out into
the glittering firmament.
And if I don't reach to it,
doesn't matter.
It just doesn't matter.

But
I am almost gone,
when nothing
happens at all.

It won't be the same ever,
I ought to know.

Page of Blood

A page
that remained
unscribbled.

A deep void of desire
that remained
unfulfilled.

A soaring crescendo of voices
that dived into
oblivion.

A searing song of emancipation
that lost all
syllables.

A craving ecstasy of dignity
that lost all
respect.

A common journey of life
that remained elusive
uncharted,
unwalked.

A red page of blood
that remained
unwritten.

Coalesce

The bloody musings
dissolve
into my
blank paper.

Hushed into
the wordless,
the silent babble
of tornado
dies.

The shimmering chimes
are tangled.

Inaudibly hissing.
it is only me
who hears solitude.

I evanesce into
mists of alphabets,
lost in the
dissipated details.

Around me,
there are

shallow pools of
crimson blood
that seem
coalescing into nothing.

The vacant air
snows into
indifference.

The hoarse cry
rains in the
graveyard.

I see
dead mourning
over
the endless agony.

Empty and drained,
yet I read the forbearance
of my countrymen—

To redden the
blank slates once again.

Solitude buried
hope rekindled.

Blood can't coalesce
into nothing.

City of Death

I am passing
over nothing.

Aimlessly
flying there,
floating here.

Houses, roads and pavements
my city delineates
bomb splinters
blood splashes.

Guns and graves
bullets and blasts
circle up the lanes.

Ruthless shadows
spineless silhouettes
hopeless hopes,
I am passing over her.

The gory smoke
fills my eyes,
I see everyone
in tears.

Doused in embers
Char-Chinari is mute.
Dal Lake peers into me,
asking for
love unrequited.

The waves of Jhelum
hurry its gospels,
as *Zainakadal* wears
the nostalgic look.

Worn out *Hari-Parbat*
couldn't fathom
the silent betrayal.

I hear voices,
choked cords—
fragile and frail
bathed in blood,
damned to despair.

Hailstorm of bullets
broken icicles now,
makes a freak show.

I am seeing you
gasping,
dying
without being mourned.

I am passing
over your death.

Antithesis

I am here
on this street corner.
I am calling out
you there.

The haze of shouts
blurs my entreaty.
The lamp on the pole
blinkers your vision.

The loneliness
smothers my being.
The crowds
surround you in vain.

Roads are blocked
for me.
Pathways of deceit
welcome you.

Angels chase me.
Ghosts stare you.

I am bound to
stand and wait

You are enticed to
move and go.

I am colourless,
I am happy.

You became a chameleon,
you are sadly inhuman.

Retreat

Love sinks away,
sun drowns in stolid ocean,
waves swallow hopes.

Sands still slip
through our fingers.

We silently shout ugliness.

The ocean throws up
broken pledges,
forgotten pleas.

Convictions lose their charm,
Fighting over dead souls.

The mood dampens,
We hate each other.

Castles on the sand
are washed away.

The dreams behind
are cold and black.

Call back the sailors,
let feelings taste slumber.

Dawn is quite far away . . .

Sulaiman

The wind across the vale
raining blood.

The ash strewn paths
weeping.

The shimmering lakes
crying.

The cindering chinars
shivering.

The day never rising
over the horizon.

The sand drifting
like black snow—

Stinging the hearts and
blinding our faith,

Burying the live souls and
vacant houses.

In this stark whisper
the rocks
wear our pain,
the rains
feel our pangs.

Lifeless Life in slow motion
Stands on the *Sulaiman*,
with its soul in the Dal
trying to sing a song—
Walo Ha Baaghvaanoa Naw Baharuk Nav Paida
Ker . . .